SUSPENSION OF A SECRET
IN ABANDONED ROOMS

PORTLAND  OREGON

Suspension of a Secret in Abandoned Rooms

by
Joshua Marie Wilkinson

Introduction *by* Jane Miller

Published by Pinball Publishing 2005
1003 SE Grant Street
Portland, OR 97214
www.pinballpublishing.com

© 2005 Joshua Marie Wilkinson
All rights reserved. This book may not be reproduced in whole or in part, in any form, without written permission from the author and/or the publisher.

ISBN 0-9721926-4-6

First Edition

Book Design by Laura Brian
Printed by Pinball Publishing
Cover Illustration by Egon Schiele. *Seated Nude*. (Kallir D. 519) Watercolor and crayon. 17.5" X 12.5" (44.5 X 31.8 cm). Private collection, photo courtesy Galerie St. Etienne, New York.

~ Table of Contents ~

Introduction *by* Jane Miller..................................8

Pictures Inside the Mattress
Before Your Brothers Are Dead............................10

Engines & Lovers...18

The Bridge in Győr...24

Skeletons & Kites...32

The Room of Hatchets, the City of Sleep...............38

Mathematics & Corpses......................................46

I Think Words Do This to Your Body....................50

Body & Colors..58

Stationhouse Crawlspace,
Darkness & Banter...62

Floodlight & Trakl..70

Piano & Brothers..74

The Satchel of Letters...80

Acknowledgements..88

For Solan Jascha & David Rubin

Illegible this
world. Everything doubled.

~Paul Celan
(translated by John Felstiner)

Suspend return of those who part with rooms
While shadows ascent   then equally fade
Suspension of the secret in abandoned rooms
Passing of secret unknown to those who part
Day receding to dark

~ Theresa Hak Kyung Cha

~ INTRODUCTION ~

Joshua Marie Wilkinson has traveled to Egon Schiele territory, to Vienna, eastern and central Austria, western Hungary, the southern Czech Republic, and northern Italy. Schiele, son of a train stationmaster, saw and painted much of this region, and Mr. Wilkinson became absorbed, if not obsessed, with retracing Schiele's experiences. Along the way, the work of other artists and thinkers of the period, including Rilke, Wittgenstein, and Trakl, began to resonate. The result is a debut book of poetry, *Suspension of a Secret in Abandoned Rooms*.

As the doubleness of the word "suspension" in the title implies, while we are held in abeyance regarding full disclosure about the past, we have access to it magically by means of a poetic solution, in which the past, perhaps magnified, remains undissolved. If one is willing to do the difficult work of recovery, the past, Mr. Wilkinson seems to be saying, can be examined. And not only that, it might also be instructive to do so, and therefore necessary.

Such a project seems eminently valuable, given the hard times we find ourselves living in. The yield may very well be enormous. It might provide just the sort of moral uplift, or intellectual power, or guts, to see us through. In such a way, art may yet, or again, prove itself useful. His poetry makes an enormous moment of history visible, in glimpses, with associations and, at times, in a cold, clear stare:

Did you set your candles on the floor as you began to draw the trees?
To pull the shadows over the paper & follow each stitch of light
until something becomes itself
and you but follow it down.

The time may be right for a poetry that is not only imaginative, but that is also grounded in reality. "Each day you must offer yourself with words to somebody," Mr. Wilkinson says, giving great responsibility to language, and to the poor soul who is taking an affirmative stand regarding life itself. This is about as un-existential, and as unashamedly positive a viewpoint as I've seen from a poet in a while. Bravo to Joshua Marie Wilkinson for believing in this world, its history and its art. His own art might make believers of his readers who, I'm confident, will trust and follow him:

It is dusk again.
A plain-clothed woman opens a side-door
from the Monastery's basement & I slip into the passageway.

Jane Miller
Tucson, July 2004

Pictures Inside the Mattress Before Your Brothers Are Dead

From the field below. Two boys. 1918.
The war is almost words again. Coughing fits.
The painter Egon Schiele dies in his sleep & today is October 31st.
Perhaps snow or just the smell of snow is the only location.

Backwards. Curse of narratives. All the characters
all at once. The way bodies come out of the morning.
Out of the forest, together & apart.

A perfume like dust. Vienna.
Cigarette pong just lingers in the hotel lobby. Friday
nights I take the train in from Bratislava. I buy oranges
& water before sleep. The next morning my tiny notes scribbled
on the map of this city will guide me to Schiele's gone rooms.

Each day you must offer yourself with words to somebody.

The cello shoulders open the song, splitting the bow immediately.
Somebody's loft in Chicago, just your fingers on the nine keys.
You've slept till after one again. But the memory I make
is when you pull the sweater over your bruised ribs
from what music?

Every Angel…

An entire album, *The Sea & the Bells*, for the moment
when Neruda lifted-open his father's casket
& seawater gushed out.

Almost deadly birds of the soul

Like a Herzog film where workers lug the sofa upstairs
& the softly crazed king must open it
as though it were an envelope in his hands.

Call me from the middle of the night where you are.
Cradle the phone on your shoulder
as you steam open the letter.

Climb down
from the barn roof & finish the story of your chores.
Black swallows in your belly. A voice tickles your throat
from the inside, which gives the inside an outside.

There are photographs of the train station where Schiele was born.
Of the stationhouse roof in Tulln. Empire
& the wrong words for each thing I recount aloud.

Of doors opening.
Couldn't I come home with an armful of groceries
to find you in the bathtub?

Opens. With pencils & an orchard ladder.
Stolen by the boy who prepared the house
& dragged the piano out into the grass
with ropes & his brothers.

A city is a kind of gift.
Stretch the map out onto the bed
& draw it over yourself, sleepy, like a quilt.

Used to sing to me as a child, my father
out of silliness or agitation, but I never found him
in the throes of a song the way he found his mother
on the kitchen floor breathing unconscious after grammar school.

In this picture I am tearing tiny maps out of guide books:
Trieste, Cesky Krumlov, Györ & folding them into
my pocket at the station.
A woman glances up at the light & I can see the train hissing
before I can hear it.

Each painting begins. The limb of some schoolboy or prostitute,
an unsmiling patron, two girls, your lover Wally, you or your wife.

An elderly woman with the body of a nun
boards the train before Budapest,
sits across from me coming from Ljubljana
& crosses herself as it lumbers out of the station.

Eight months over the Slovak-Austrian border on evening
& Saturday morning trains.
Toppled buildings upright. Rain.

When there's a figure there's never a landscape.
The opposite is true also.
Border guards with little pencils & weather in the trees.

As she steps off the trolley her dress hem catches on the jamb & tears.
Wally has red wrists. Around her eyes are red too.
She carries gouache sketches of herself
to the cafés for Egon. Split is the name of the town in Dalmatia.

Empire of Dusk.
Pressburg, Budapest & Trieste. Yellow sputter
& hiss of boxcars unhinging ball sockets. Steel.

Somehow swallows nest in the creosote eaves,
flit-scatter, fall back & return.
Vienna, ~~Paris~~ & your mother's dead town, little Krumau.
You sleep where the trains sleep. Muddy thickets,
wasp hives & flapping laundry lines.

Sketching trains on the stationhouse roof after supper.
Charcoal for the engine plumes—Umbrella,
did you bring me here?

Engines & Lovers

> The gramophone record, the musical thought, the score, the waves of sound, all stand to one another in that pictorial internal relation, which holds between language & the world.
> ~ *Ludwig Wittgenstein*
> *(translated by Peter Winch)*

Picture an engine.
        Now picture its gears,
                the pins
    & sockets, the tin grease canister
              with its hummingbird nose.
Paraffin.
Turbines hum. Shuffle of men in the entry
            & a stitch
                that yields soldier sounds & a telling
        before words assemble
    from opposed cylinders, flesh
            confused, curved spoke flywheels, a pile
of clothes soiled from gardening on your knees into the evening.
                        Bits of metal cut like saw blades
                & polished like jewelry
meshed together, two bodies at the kitchen sink.
              Brahms on the gramophone
                        by the fire.

Only, an engine needs
> fluid or steam for heat, a method for cooling,
>> exhaust, a body & then a way to begin.
>>> If it's warm,
> I sleep on the back porch
>> or under the rear window on the bedroom floor
> when the bed
>> becomes too much to make.

Picture a giant steam engine
            in the basement of a textile factory.
    Austria, 1920.
                    Now imagine a schoolteacher silently pacing,
inspecting the busted engine. Enter four men. Give them hammers
& give them each a number
                    say, 6 or 2. Each man must strike the engine
        with his hammer
                    & number
                            & the engine will tick
        shake & begin again.

Dear L,
Since you have left for your cabin in the fjords I have pulled
                          the carpet away & rolled it neatly
                                behind the house.
            After the black leaves are dampened
   I spread them over the floorboards, my bedroom
reeks of tea & reminds me, wet, of you. Now, tell the story
       of the engines
       you built, the giant
       propeller you wanted so badly
       to fit into a flying machine. You had men
              build you a special combustion chamber
    for diesel & rotary tests. Failed.

                       Or that tiny machine
     for measuring the blood & breath
of mine-blown soldiers, the second war's amputees.
                What did the blood return you to?
Why are you hiding from me?

Nineteen weeks.
        Your one
    note to my every third letter.
            Even if all my words
   cross me,
       if your shame doesn't keep me shut
      I am done with all the parts of me
              you tried to fix.
    It has dripped rain for a week straight.
My thoughts just
    correct themselves bickering, one
after another, until I take the late train into the city
            to undo the stickiness
of your absence. This doesn't usually work.

Grey woodmice have burrowed into
      the soggy carpet behind the house
   though mostly I can't hear them at all.

The Bridge in Győr

The first boy awakens under the butcher paper to Egon's laughter.
The studio is filled with dusk & Wally collects the clothes
of the children scattered about. Something has happened
inside the room, but nobody will speak into it.

Then reports from the neighbor girl beating two rugs at a time.
Her arms flail.

To make sense of it I board a Slovak-Hungarian train,
reading McGrath's letters aloud.
Across buckled streets & fields of mud I come
to the bridge in Győr or where the bridge
might have been in 1913.

Teenagers ditch their muddy bikes in the shrubs
& drag on cigarettes this morning where
the east stream slurs to swan drift & murk.

Nightfall. Trainstation derelict light.
Hungarian voices fill the room from below.
Old water. Only, here in this book in my lap
are the wooden suspension beams that rise for
crossing into the evening, all afternoon
it's taken me to find a concrete Russian imposter.

An accordion of tiny birds over the house. Finishing
myself in this portrait. Coarse light. Father's fingers in my mouth.
I used to rob his gold buttons to melt them in the firepit. In the hangar.

Last night again, boyghosts whispering Slovak
& snow fell in the shape of a city.
A brass key to squeeze into the outside door lock,
I found my breath for nothing. Even the muffled plunkety-plung-
plunk of the child's piano is quiet.

Somewhere in Saskatchewan, still 1913.
My grandmother is born & Egon Schiele in Krumau
is younger than I am now, doing his best work.

People said when he entered a room with a mirror
Schiele would just stare at his own face
for several minutes before saying a word to anyone.

Bratislava Transcript. Sunday in February. On
the telephone telling my father about Egon Schiele:

no—a painter, well…mostly bodies—
no—
like people, self-portraits, Yeah—
& landscapes, small towns in Czechoslovakia,
Austro-Hungarian Empire. No, only about 10 years, in 1918.
World War One. Yeah, only twenty-eight,
but something like three thousand paintings survived.
Just as the war ended, yeah.
No, no—
Spanish Influenza, killed two million.

Listen when a body is quiet, when it startles
& its racket casts a line into you.

Before. No, before.
With the cats in the barn loft sleeping.
Wally burns her letters
over the sink before her bath each night.

If.
Eight boys. The second boy begins mumbling
in his sleep.

No one will confirm his father coming home with syphilis
but it takes Egon's three brothers.

There is no history of your mouth, speech.
Word this properly.
The way your eyes claim the body you're sketching.

Forgetting it. I haven't gone far enough
                without you. This war.
        Dreamed open.
            A window has me speaking.
                          Umbrella?
                    Did you…?
                          Cigarettes

in your hat. Still, here, again is the war & I can't even hear it.
Earth buzzing invisibly.

Instructions for the fourth boy: Heave the sacks of peat off the truck.
Stack them neatly along the fence, then go home.

1906. In Klosterneuburg Schiele is fifteen & sketches
the town from here. Here exactly where Wittgenstein
set everything down
after the war to work in the garden of the Monastery.
After Schiele is dead.
                              Rainer Maria sits at a table
with another bearded man who speaks with his teeth. *I've
forgotten now where, and they were saying something
about something white.*

        You won't know
        what kind of room it is until
                the hired boy
        with a pouch
        of tiny tools
        rinses his hands quietly in the sink
                & begins picking the first lock.

Great Falls. Here
is my father at the levee as a boy. Mostly I watch his legs.

Egon had seen me a few times chatting with friends
under the ferris wheel & would I
come home, have lunch &, for a drawing, undress?
His hands were white. I held mine out.
After school with oranges, coffee candy.

So yes I know the story of the girl,
of the girl's cantankerous father & of the boy
who so loved Egon he slept in a pile of books to pretend
it was Schiele's body in the shed of his uncle's orchard.

It is dusk again.
A plain-clothed woman opens a side-door
from the Monastery's basement & I slip into the passageway.

Skeletons & Kites

All this rain, Glossop, England. The ground
         is puddles, muck. I awake
   this morning to grapefruit juice & hot tea
                think of you
                          lacing your boots,
            carrying
                   a yellow kite out into the road
   determined as a child up the hill.
                             Whistling
         Schubert exactly
                 & muttering
           the pack horses of Iceland into
   arithmetic means.

Even your teachers will find you
    illegible. Augustine
  in your fidgeting—
    If there is a single equation
        to rid me
      of my longing
    & if I can summon its spell
      then will the confession
         outlast its confessor?

Dear Egon,
Another cat has died. This one
I found in the road on my way to the schoolhouse
yesterday morning. It seems to be scrawny enough
that to extract its bones would be easier than
the plump farmcats I wrote of before. Just today
I wrapped it in newspaper & put it in the icebox.
Why am I so squeamish? Borax will whiten
& preserve the bones. A milky paste
to reassemble its skeleton.

It is an intricate fingerwork (surgeon's scalpel
& paring knife) everything must be precise.
Orchestras shudder in my mind as I pull the clotted fur
& skin away from the ribs of its body. Imagine—
I will finally put down the chalk & stop speaking
to the children. The day after tomorrow, I'll bring in
the wooden dowels for them & nylon to build box kites.

It feels right to ask you here if you'll come back.
Was I really so horrid last April? You know
the simplest words always spoil my meaning. Missing
you rings deep in my jaw. Some poison.

I even dreamt that the neighbors had come over
for tea after supper to listen to the gramophone.
When I open the icebox, kittens too many to count
begin mewing & mewing. Each

succession of notes spins inside me, focuses me.
Tearing the ears back, the soft skin of the nose
the tiniest fur of the chin & paws is, of course,
the hardest part. An itty-bitty horrible mess.
It's the way you want to be gentle but
the scalpel becomes a pickaxe. Though
in the morning the children will set down their things
& gather oblong around its skeleton.

The Room of Hatchets, the City of Sleep

A long walk out into the wheat & the scarecrow flaps up into
starlings.

Some children carry ripe oranges to the abandoned airplane hangar.
Through Hornet's Nest Gully,
around a little trampled path along the side,
hand the paper bag in & slip around the peeled back hunk
of aluminum hangar wall.

Listen when they open each other with laughter, it loosens the paint
& spills into your neck.
A little girl has words bigger than her body. Bigger.

Here the second boy is speaking as if in a missive
from the orchard washbasin but without paper.

Will you pull this off & draw what the mirror returns to you?
Upstairs out of the basement. The dog lunging
after angry birds in the wind.

I can imagine music without moving my teeth too,
but in that case the notes are much ghostlier, more blurred & less pronounced.

Wally's diction is precise, almost impossible. Require
something of me. Command me to stay.

Once she said simply, *more yellow*
& Egon walked into the garden as if for a cigarette.

Photographing myself endlessly, in keeling German
to strangers or alone on trains.
The woman with the mole's eyes holds up her arm
like the number 4 & her red dress is a quilt on fire.
This painting scores my sleep.

schoolgirls sleeping
schoolboys sleeping and stemmed

I will dream you
Draw you

Six screens of shade & brown light almost yellow.
A tiny lever in your wrist, a perfect spine, just invisible.
Voices & napping I dream back Vienna,
of the third train station to tiny Tulln. River grass, bright
wet sunlight.

The nude women from the severed triptych with their backs turned.
Their hair pinned up. Under the photograph of the cut sketch it reads:

PRESENT WHEREABOUTS UNKNOWN.

Dripping fingers
as if you'd come to know in secret. Painting
one hand with the other.

Born six months & thirty
kilometers apart from Schiele,
Wittgenstein loses three brothers also
but in a dissimilar sequence:
the first to Chesapeake Bay,
the second to cyanide & gin in a piano bar, 1904.
The third brother, refused by his troops,
shot himself in the throat.

World War I. Wally disappears as a nurse to Dalmatia
& Egon sketches storerooms & Russian prisoners. 1915.
This year only. The nudes have dead eyes, soft as an eyelid.
Tangled around you, your new wife Edith pulls up your smock.
What did you say to freeze it
& stop the bodies from one another?
Rename, reinscribe,
hack out the pieces. The hatchet hacks.

City of hangnails & doorlocks.
Which shovel did you carry up the stairs & for what?

Once we drove all night & all day & into the next night.
Little wolves seemed to jump into the wheels of the car.
I woke outside Kansas City & asked if
the sun was going up or coming down.

It's just as you said, the phone is a trick,
an echo of your body in the moment you've hung up.
That stapled-shut silence.

Of waking up between your naked shoulders.
The hot early evening rain floods the streets. Tucson.
A mess of artichokes & white cheese on the floor.

Here is the burnt open field in Oregon where we've pulled over,
my hand under your dress. The way you open & close your eyes.

Three paintings of your little sister Gerti in 1910 & I can almost,
among the metal rinse tubs of fixative & stop-bath,

hear her wiggling out of her dress in the darkroom.
Sniff-kissing your ribcage & skinny elbows.

Here are six thin brushes,
a little tray of water muddied turquoise.
Penciled ghost.
            Her almost-body in crayon,
in carroty gouache.

Kneecaps stained.
Faint green water strokes for the sternum.

The darkroom key tucked in my leather boot.
Stick out your elbow like the roof of a house.

Mathematics & Corpses

Before the smeared-over blackboard he stands
& mumbles silently, wearing the same tweed jacket
& ashen look.

Egon,
This ghost opens its mouth as if to speak & just—
turns me, your breath on my face
to the park where the boys linger
& leer each other
into the open shadows.
Language is always a description and.

Just below the Arctic Circle a plane crashes.
A second
                      plane lifts off in Húsavik
to uncover the cause
of the first crash
& crashes also.   What
                            mathematics could
                                  _____this?

        Flickering marquee & blockade
                      missing something—
    laughing lies out of their mouths…

        When what's untellable becomes
      an expression of inverted letters.
          Z is for A,
                U for F
                      & S for H until
                            the first thirteen letters
            of the alphabet
        are ghosted beneath the second.

I'm stuffing
all these
envelopes
into a wooden
box under
the desk.
If words
are corpses
I must,
scrambled
in code,
name what
this longing
is like
& what
this longing
is not.

I Think Words Do This to Your Body

Three girls are already gossiping.
One at a time & then all together.
The one with the red shoes hushes the others
& holds her mouth just so
until my own breathing becomes a train.

The scent of the city lures us back together,
finding ourselves in these bodies, in this billiard hall of rusted pipes.

Egon, I still have three things to ask you
& three things to ask you to carry, though
what's what escapes me.

Did you set your candles on the floor as you began to draw the trees?
To pull the shadows over the paper & follow each stitch of light
until something becomes itself
& you but follow it down.

I think words do this to your body.

Clatter from my sleep in the basement, in the attic.
Each room. Even the kitchen is dead with refrigerator buzz
& the window I never think to wash.
Rooms just decide things as we come in,
before we've even taken off our coats
or pulled the sheets from the bed.

Halloween drizzle. I walk west through Vienna,
& place three oranges at the grave.
Your wife Edith & the baby that died in her womb.

I think body this to your words do.

Now
crawl back under the house
& wait for my signal
at dusk.

I know
the path to the trainhouse,
you won't need
your eyes.

Only
if your
promise
takes me on
to Vienna with you.

Dear Egon,
I am writing to tell you that the house here in Krumau
is ready for you. There's a piano in the studio
though keys are missing. I will drag it out with my brothers if you say.
Also, a handsome girl lives next door.
She's a dancer with broad shoulders & a flat nose like a boxer's.

Woods can be a city.

The string of a teabag on your finger, a child's hand
                          in your jacket pocket.
Tiny sparrow
           trapped in the shower
after you've brought the plants in for watering
                                & fallen asleep.

At fifteen my dad used to drive out of dry counties in Arkansas
to get a crate of liquor for his best friend's father,
a tinman named Leo who couldn't get out of bed without first
lighting a cigarette. Hacking his *Goddamn cops
are swine* & *Goddamn this trick knee.*
I imagine his tender way of humming,
undressing & crawling into the unmade Murphy bed each morning
too inebriated to barter with the aluminum hawkers who'd ruin him
before the smoke or cirrhosis could.
Green ashtray at the knot of her elbow filled with menthol butts,
Donna, irritated, finally just gets up & does it for him.
Her gapped teeth & cracked red lipstick at his collar,
she can see him looking & not looking.
A kicked dent in the wall & every two or three minutes
another John walks by.
My father buckling his belt hears the woman nearly giggling
& the man's whiskery chuckle following her in.

This long mirror I find myself inside
your soft Krumau, wintered.
Colors of new teeth, a man's gums, pumpkin rot.

Is your hand drawn back to strike? to shield the neck?
to make secret?
Your right shoulder pulled up to your face,
one long black browline furrowed over the glare of your eyes
yet pleading with
              what desire rids us of,
what it casts off & returns for. Returning for.

Body & Colors

Egon,
Cormorants again. Again, the dream of the waterwheel. Again
the notched slats misshapen in rot beyond repair
& all my penciling work mouthed to deaf eyes,
absurd as the curlews Tommy rows me out to see
in the afternoon & I become furious & sort of peaceful at once. Not

in the dream, but out on the water there is a little island of mud
where I could get some thinking done if Tommy would
build a thatch hut for me, but he refuses. The man with two
elk hounds closes his eyes to slits
& gives each bird a gesture, a wrist flick
& nod that seem unintelligible.

The greens of the Killary Coast in Ireland are a dialect of birds:
Northern Divers, Oyster Catchers, Puffins & Terns
& I've put all the demands of my bestiary
of propositions away for the sake of six
or seven colors which require all my attention.

You'll laugh, but Tommy doesn't believe in
his organs, only the bruises from boxing with the boys upstairs
which cover the insides of his forearms, the small of his back.
Something about the way they deteriorate from purple to a mud-yellow
& vanish, never reappearing in the same places or as the same shapes.

Silence is only the dimmed
        fullness of a thousand new sounds. Paddling
in a bog. Tree drip & fog drip,
                even the prow dripping.
                        The body's stickiness
                    & the body's taste.
From upstairs the boys' bright racket
                    compels me to leave.

The one photograph I have of you
holding
your hat,
patting down your hair, coat sopping.
It's sutured to the memory of you
in my
doorway,
though in the picture
you are at the trainstation still in Vienna.

                    For months
      on the rug of the front room
with Mozart, I would open
            my eyes feeling that you had
     slipped in.
              Your body,
yes, but first blow out the candle.

STATIONHOUSE CRAWLSPACE
DARKNESS, & BANTER

Something shrill breaks in the eaves & I want this to be finished,
to be back in Alaska. Searching with Solan for black bears
rummaging currants on the train track canopied
by foliage. But something cracks, sprinkles sawdust
from the warped eaves & locates me.

Spigot steam. Washing my feet at the fogged-in beach, freezing.

What time did the news arrive?
Where were you before it happened? No, before.

It's 1913, the year of the bridge & the twin of this woman
is holding her lavender smock shut with her right hand,
only the inside of her arm,
                the nape of her neck are listening.

Another ghost in the room
through the sounds of another alphabet.

Always a woman dressing or undressing.

Someone whispering into your mouth.
Not *to* exactly. Not *for* exactly either.

The noise of crates dragging
             soon after you left.
    Cigar smoke,
              sundust hang together
                         in the sawmill.
    & lumber steams in the east-light.

         Dry laughter of dogs.

You said,
carry the keys no matter what
         because some rooms
      are guarded by other rooms & shadows
                         kill the breeze.
Children disappear like butterflies
      into the overgrown plum copse below.

Your hands, Egon.
The one thing you could paint, you didn't.
A mattress upright behind you in the cell.
The peeling wall that you begin to trace.
Brushes rinsed in the toilet water.

I come back to them in the subway at forty-something street:
The prison cell watercolors. Neulengbach, 1912.
A girl or the girl's father wanted you.
& here I am on the train in my own reflection thinking
mornings I want them to bring a robin's three blue eggs
to the lead slot in the prison cell door.

Gather up the children & set them into the street. Scatter out.

The stationhouse darkness smells of bricks
& of the kittens born three days ago
 in the crawlspace under the platform.
My father is in his full train uniform collar, jacket & stationmaster cap,
but naked from the waist down.

Boxcars, midnight unhasp & heave off.

Gerti squirms into my wool blankets, humming to muffle the banter,
staggered banging. All my father's dirty railroad cities
& whore junctions rasp open the bud of insomnia.

I notice the bruise on the small of your back
as we lift the box of books into the overhead train compartment.
From the window onto a strange room I watch a little girl
hoist her self onto the piano bench
& poke her little chin onto a black key.

Ivy-paths & apples in the sink with ants.

The railroad was invented
some 350 years later to explain
why things disappear

I have a scar
on my wrist from I don't know what.

Floodlight & Trakl

A strange one in war.
To a body anything can happen,
Like a brick. Too obvious to say.
But all horror came from it.
  —George Oppen

Dear Egon,
Twilight & your death comes
      for me in little packages of chocolate & cigarettes
         which I hoard.
            Though, pictures are beginning
      to form & if I can outlast the floodlight
               of this river I will return home
      to build you something nice.

Each day Russia comes forth & forth. Each day the war can't
      fathom itself.
Gross miscalculations send us back to Krakow
up the Vistula. Paris is
      whispered apart in flames. Rumors too much to
      bear, the mouths
& fingertips retell. But the poet Trakl has written & asked me
         to visit him in hospital there.

> *The blueness of my eyes has gone out this night,*
> *The red gold of my heart. O how tranquil the light shone.*
> *Your blue mantle enfolded the sinking man;*
> *Your red mouth sealed your friend's dark derangement.*

The yellow night of combat hissing. Fool's song in the square.
A whole city battered open, so through it, will you come?

There is a floodlight
twice the size of my body
& as we troll the Polish shoreline out of Galicia
I shine this great spear into the bottomless forests,
into the river's villages for the gunners to aim.

Once I saw lovers, a pack of wolves
                      vanish, a man waving something,
    giant birds
        lift into flight, tugged off like puppets. When the river broke
    into four directions
        my floodlight meant nothing.

But there is a solitude like perfected noise if I can
              steady it. Of course there are no birds at night.
              That you kiss the muscles
    on the nape of my neck, unbutton
                    your buttons,
the flesh of my shoulders sings in the morning when I flop into bed.
News of your death has hexed my body, yet I
                tug & scold myself in the latrine.

What I could to your mother, I wrote. My body & this
war have so much in common.

Piano & Brothers

Lower East Village. A different two boys. 1998.
Together they push their mattress underneath
the black grand piano in their studio apartment.

One boy gently loosens the keys
from inside the instrument.
Tiny hammers, tines.

Phantom limb. Cut your heart down into a bird from the tree
      & the snow is fallout eaten by the river.
            Death is this postcard. When.

    Stimmen, I cannot divide the question
from my body.
      The bright bleat of this clarinet
            like the clatter of sunshine.

Will there be weather when we arrive in Krakow?

      What can it mean that fire appears
            in my dreams only
      if I doze off in the afternoon?

The same two boys.
The first is stage-side at the church
of St. Philip in Louisville.
The other boy keeps
disappearing into the performance.
One cello & a viola.
Rachel sits at the church piano keys hearing it
with her wrists. The boys make a tape
of all the sounds & disassemble a piano in their studio.
They use crochet needles, a child's toy mallet,
an old ski glove & bedsheets tied end to end
& woven into the hammers,
anything to yank or loosen.
Twelve microphones record this. Eventually
the song disintegrates into an idling garbage truck,
static blasts, eighth note shaker & snare beats,
another violin being pulled slowly apart
by the fingers of one boy
while the other plays it patiently.

Egon,
I can see it in the evening:
                     death by musket, death by
     song & approximation,
             death by light, by kissing the key
into the desk's secret drawer. Tiny hush.
                    Fragment.

Death by the steamed open
               envelope, by woodthrush,
                             by the blunt end of the shovel,
by salt barrel & the steam engine hissing itself apart.
      Death by missing the body itself. By looking for too long.
         By aperture,
                  death by stammering over the bridge
      from the cathedral. Death

                       by piano drop & ocean & by hiding things
  from yourself. This could. Rife fields & bring dreams.

The Satchel of Letters

I am writing from the outhouse by candlelight
& father may at any moment burst in.

My pillow no longer smells of you or, worse, I've nearly
forgotten your scent. The bedroom window rattles
& I sleep shaky in fits.

I fear that these letters will not reach you,
that the messenger boy's already betrayed me

& reads this with yellow eyes before he shakes the bag out
into the ravine from underneath the bridge.

The pitched roof of the pharmacy gives the rest of the black painting
the slightest glow where the red fronts of houses are nearly brown.
The sky & blue river are flat.
The bluish shutters of a small house are thrown open to the moonlight.

Black silhouettes could be anything but the figures I see.
A couple quarreling or stretching after love in the summer darkness,
sharing a cigarette at the window.

You fall asleep thirsty with your mouth open.
But I picture you again, at the kitchen window sewing white feathers
into your fire-spinning dress, your cat Texas asleep in the sink
& even music tricks me, brings you back.

Her dark hands the color of oxmeat, a girl
mumbling Czech, leads me into Krumau.
The castle paunches over the town split with ice.
Here where the old rooms want to find us in you.

All night the specter of you haunts me in this little town.
How you'd stroll in the autumn, a bright orange from Naples
in your coat pocket.
Ninety-one years later I return to the houses you painted here.

The freezing March hooks in. I can't hear you
in the cobbles of this place,
but something of your open hand lingers simply
like the scent of bridgefrost.

Late in the evening I get this spoked feeling
that one thing holds the smallest parts of me together
& if I say too much, speak too loudly, they will all come to pieces.

Rachel,
It's as if the cello strain could open the sketchbook & know me
over its pulled notes & constellations.

The clumsy folio of drawings is under his arm.
Squatted down, Egon speaks with the pregnant women in the
waiting room,

But he slips out to find the basement
stairwell. The song begins here, just your fingers on the nine keys.

Two morticians work silently, one at a huge metal sink,
one at a metal clipboard. Schiele lies, *This is my sister…*
& motions to the body on the table. The doctors vanish.

Egon sets his folio
on the table
beside the dead girl's bluish thigh.
The room reeks of alcohol,
vaguely of corn or bad wine.

He props the girl's wooden hands
above her flattened body
so that the fingers touch as if in a dead
prayer & he sketches her
asleep on water.

If, on the center of the bridge, you close one eye the edges disappear.

Hot shower steam that hangs over the sink.
I can see your ribs & spine when you walk around the room in a towel.
Your hair pulled up wet, your kneecaps pink.

There is three of me, one
in the bedroom with you, shaving at the mirror. One
in the story of its noise bustling. The third reading it slowly back
aloud now while you drift off to sleep.

ACKNOWLEDGEMENTS

Grateful acknowledgment is made to the editors of *Versal*, *Spork*, *Harness*, and to the Rella Lossy Chapbook Award in which sections of this book length poem appeared in significantly different forms.

ACKNOWLEDGEMENTS OF ITALICIZED EXCERPTS

Page 12 - Rainier Maria Rilke (translated by Stephen Mitchell)
Page 29 - Cole Swensen
Page 40 - Ludwig Wittgenstein (translated by Peter Winch)
Page 41 - Susan Howe
Page 68 - Cole Swensen
Page 71 - Georg Trakl (translated by Alexander Stillmark)

SPECIAL THANKS TO:

Laura and Austin, Casey and Chip for believing in this book. Mom, Dad, Jeffrey. My teachers: Tom Williams, Bruce Beasley, Colleen McElroy, Yusef Komunyakaa, Mark Doty, Carolyn Forché, Alison Hawthorne Deming, Boyer Rickel, Jon Anderson, Jason Brown, Tenney Nathanson, Charlie Bertsch, and Eric Hayot, Bin Ramke and Eleni Sikelianos—infinite thanks to Jane Miller for seeing this book through its earliest forms to its present one. Frances Sjoberg and Christine Krikliwy at the Poetry Center in Tucson. Warmest thanks to Zach Zulauf and Scott Lindsay, Theresa Vu, Lisa Schumaier, Gwyneth Scally, Dougie Weber, Adrienne Walser, J. Wesley Fullerton, Tim Sanders, Fran Varian, Coy King, Sara Zane, Paul Harding, and Termite. Allison Maletz, Leah Breen, Geneva Ley, Frank Montesonti, Jason Zuzga, and Richard Siken. Tim Rutili, Jim Becker, Ben Massarella, Joe Adamik. Fuad bin Rahmat, Ricardo Zozimo, and Rachel Smith, Julie Doxsee, Duncan Barlow, Paul Fattaruso, J'Lyn Chapman, Gregory Howard, Marty Riker, Christina Mengert. And open thanks to the band Rachel's for their record *Music for Egon Schiele* which scored the drafting of this book for nearly four years. Endless thanks to John and Mary Felstiner. David and Solan: "To know that one does not write for the other… to know that writing compensates for nothing, sublimates nothing, that it is precisely there where you are not—this is the beginning of writing" (Barthes, "Inexpressible Love," 1977).